SMART COMEB

STUPID QUESTIONS

by

RICHARD PORTEUS

Illustrated by

CHARLES GOLL

CCC PUBLICATIONS

Published by

CCC Publications
9725 Lurline Avenue
Chatsworth, CA 91311

Manufactured in the United States of America

Cover & Interior art by Charles Goll
Cover/Interior production by Oasis Graphics
ISBN: 1-57644-040-0

If your local bookstore is out of stock, copies of this book may be obtained by mailing check or money order for $5.95 per book (plus $2.50 to cover postage and handling) to:
CCC Publications; 9725 Lurline Avenue, Chatsworth, CA 91311

Pre-publication Edition - 10/96
First Printing - 1/97
Second Printing - 4/97
Third Printing - 7/97
Fourth Printing - 9/97
Fifth Printing - 3/98
Sixth Printing - 7/98
Seventh Printing - 9/98
Eighth Printing - 1/99
Ninth Printing - 4/99
Tenth Printing - 9/99
Eleventh Printing - 12/00
Twelfth Printing - 3/02

INTRODUCTION

Anyone can ask a stupid question ONCE in a while. It happens when the answer to what you're asking is totally obvious to the other person. This can occur anywhere at any place. The rest of the time you don't LOOK stupid; you don't ACT stupid; you don't DRESS stupid. Nice going!

Is there a quick cure for stupiditis? You bet! Look at the examples in this book. They will draw your attention to the MOST OBVIOUS stupid questions that you should avoid.

Also, after looking at the pictures and reading the comebacks, you could be the proud announcer of your own outrageous, sarcastic, but appropriate responses to other people's stupid questions.

Whether you are young or old, male or female, rich or poor, our hope is that you will find this book both helpful and cathartic in a fun and humorous way.

IS THIS ALL YOU HAVE?
NO. I COULD POP HOME AND GET SOME FOOD FROM MY KITCHEN.

EXCUSE ME, DO YOU WORK HERE?
NO. THIS IS MY HALLOWEEN COSTUME.
SLOPPY LUBE
ENGINES FOR DUMMIES

FOR ME!?
NO. JUST SMELL THEM. THEN I HAVE TO RETURN THEM TO THE FLORIST.

DO YOU WANT A BAG?
NO, I'LL JUST TAKE IT OUT IN MY SHOE.
COFFEE
.75 1.00 1.25
TEA
.50 1.00 1.50
MILK
.75 1.25 1.75
LAPD
SPECIAL
RHUBARB
TARTS
75¢ 50¢ 25
FREE
NEW!
MR.
COOKIE

DO YOU THINK SHE WANTS TO GO OUT?
NO. I THINK IT'S AN AEROBIC EXERCISE FOR DOGS.
CAPT. JANEWAY
DR WHO

BOSTON
DOES THIS BUS GO TO BOSTON?
NO. BOSTON IS REALLY OUR CODE NAME FOR DETROIT.
UNIVER OF BOSTO
BOARD BOSTON BUS HERE

BLOWOUT SALE!!
FREEZER
UNITS
WHITE MODEL ONL
CAN I GET IT IN ANY OTHER COLOR?
YES. ALL WHITE AND VERY WHITE.
HI! I'M
100% WHITE
50% WHITE

HOW'S YOUR HEADACHE NOW?
GREAT! IT'S THE BEST ONE I'VE EVER HAD! I WANT TO KEEP IT FOREVER!

IS HE FRIENDLY?
SURE! THIS IS HOW HE SMILES.
GAS CO
BEWARE OF EVIL, VICOUS DOG
AND OWNER

CAN I BUY A POUND OF HAM?
NO. WE PREFER YOU BORROW IT.
ASK ABOUT OUR LIVER (WE DARE YOU!)
1.06 lb
BLOOD SAUSAGE (YUM!) 1.06 lb

OH! IS DINNER READY?
NO. I'M ARRANGING A STILL LIFE TO PAINT.

IS THE WATER COLD, DEAR?
NO, MOTHER, I ALWAYS SHAKE MYSELF DRY!
TV

DO YOU THINK IT'S CLOGGED?
NO. I THINK THE TIDE IS COMING IN.
MOE
PLUMBIN
AND
AIR COND

FRAME FRENZY
THE WORLD'S LARGEST DEALER IN PICTURE FRAMES
"WE'LL FRAME YOU!
DO YOU HAVE A FRAME FOR THIS PICTURE?
NO. WHAT WE SELL HERE IS EXPENSIVE FIREWOOD.
0 $
0 $

ANY LUCK?
YES, BUT I ATE THEM AS SOON AS I CAUGHT THEM.

WOULD YOU LIKE A SEAT?
NO. I'M TRYING TO BREAK THE RECORD FOR STANDING WITH BOXES ON A SUBWAY.
GIFTS R US!
GIFTS R US!

AND WOULD YOU LIKE THIS DELIVERED?
NO. I'LL BRING MY KITCHEN IN HERE.
SOLD
FROST FREE!
ENERGY RATING 9.5
WHATEVER THAT MEANS
$1! (NO QUESTIONS ASKED!)

DID YOU HURT YOURSELF FALLING?
NO, LADY, I LOOKED THIS WAY BEFORE I FELL.
Coming to this Site
ANOTHER EXPENSIVE SKYSCRAPER FROM
DANGER

IS THAT HOW MUCH I WEIGH, DOCTOR?

NO. THAT'S WHAT I CHARGE PER VISIT.

DEAD MAN WALKING

STICK INSECT

TV MODEL

JOE 6-PACK

PRO. EATER

OVER THE HILL

WILL THIS BE CASH?
FOOD VILLE
EXPRESS
100 ITEMS OR LESS
NO. I WANT YOU TO DONATE IT TO ME.
MAGAZINES
FOOD VILLE 100% YAK'S MILK
GOLDFISH
SHARK
TUNA

BASEMENT PARKING LEVEL
DO YOU KNOW WHERE YOU PARKED?
ARE YOU SURE?
GOING UP?
LEVATOR
UP ONLY
NO. TODAY IS THE DAY WE GO SIDEWAYS.
I ♥ WORK
I ♥ WORK
RESERVED

IS THE COFFEE HOT?
NO. WE SERVE IT FROZEN ON A STICK.
EAT
MENU
TEXAS
TODAY'S SPECIAL
ROADKILL STEW
GUESS OUR MYSTERY MEAT! WIN PRIZE!!

WOULD YOU LIKE TO SEE THE REST OF THE HOUSE?
NO. WE JUST WANT TO BUY THE KITCHEN.
A TO Z REALTY

ARE YOU GOING OUT?
NO, I'M PRACTICING HOW TO OPEN AND CLOSE DOORS.

WHAT CAN I DO FOR YOU, YOUNG MAN?
HAIRCUTS
TRIM $10
BUZZCUT $12
CREWCUT
SCALPING
I CAME IN TO GET MY PANTS PRESSED.

IS THE MUSIC TOO LOUD?
NOT IF YOU'RE PLAYING IT FOR THE PEOPLE DOWNTOWN!

ARE YOU GOING TO MAIL THOSE LETTERS?
SING SOMETHING ALFALFA
NO. I'M GOING TO MAKE A LETTERS AND TOMATO SANDWICH WITH THEM.

HAS THIS SEAT BEEN TAKEN?
NO, LADY, IT'S STILL HERE.

INTERESTED IN A NEW CAR, SIR?
NO. I'M TRYING TO GET IDEAS ON HOW TO BUILD ONE OF MY OWN.
BUY ME!!
NO! BUY ME!!
LUXURY MODEL
BUY THIS MODEL AND KEEP OUR SALESTAFF IN LUXURY

XEDOS
SQUIRTING CARNATION FREE WITH EVERY RENTAL
CAN I RENT A TUXEDO?
NO. I'M SAVING THEM FOR A YARD SALE.
TERRI'S TUXEDO RENTAL

NOW, WHO COULD THAT BE KNOCKING?
MAYBE IT'S A PROFESSIONAL DOOR KNOCKER.
U. OF Z.

CAN I GET YOU SOMETHING, SIR?
NO. I JUST LIKE TO GO AROUND SMELLING FOOD.
BUS YOUR OWN TRAY
LIKE, WE'RE NOT YOUR SLAVE, OK?
FREE! BLIMPO ACTION FIGURE WITH EVERY 40 OZ. DRINK
BLIMPO BURGER

WANT ME TO TAKE OUT THE GARBAGE?
NO. HIDE IT IN THE GUEST ROOM.

ARE YOU STILL ON THE PHONE?
NO. I'M MASSAGING MY FACE.
YANNI RULES
YANNI SUCKS

WHAT'S GOOD FOR A HEADACHE?
SOMETHING THAT WILL MAKE IT GO AWAY.
PHARMAC
PLACE ORDER HERE
GOOD FOR HEADACH
SECTION
HEAD-ACHE? TRY THIS
NEW
MIRACLE CURE
WONDER DRUG
CURES HEADACHE FAST!
PLEASE HAVE YOUR HEADACHE INSURANCE CARD

WAITING FOR A TAXI, LADY?
NO. I'M PROTECTING YOUR SIGN FROM THIEVES.
GETTA TAXI CO.

OH! ARE YOU UP, DEAR?
NO. YOUR HUSBAND IS STILL ASLEEP. I'M HIS EVIL TWIN.
FiDo

ARE YOU OPEN?
NO. I'M SITTING HERE BECAUSE I LIKE THE VIEW.
NEXT WINDOW PLEASE
NEXT WINDOW PLEASE
PLEASE DO NOT SHOOT THE POSTAL WORKERS

SUBWAY
EXCUSE ME, BUT DO YOU HAVE THE CORRECT TIME?
YES.

MAIL
WHY IS THAT DOG BARKING?
PROBABLY BECAUSE HE CAN'T "MOO".

LOSE SOMETHING?
PLAY
NO. I'M LOOKING FOR A SHORTCUT TO THE BATHROOM.

CARE TO SEE A MENU?
NO SPITTING
NO. WE WANT TO GUESS WHAT YOU HAVE.

DID YOU JUST HEAR AN AWFUL NOISE?!?
YES... YOUR VOICE...

YOU LOCKED YOUR KEYS IN THE CAR AGAIN?!
NO! I'M TAKING THE DOOR OFF TO LET MORE AIR IN!

WHERE DO YOU WANT THE AIR CONDITIONER, LADY?
IN THAT TREE OUTSIDE THE WINDOW.
YES!
MOE'S
SOLD

PERHAPS YOU'D LIKE TO TRY A SMALLER SIZE?
NO. JUST GIVE ME A PAIR OF SCISSORS.
STORE WIDE CLEARANCE SALE
50% OFF
ALL STORE EMPLOYEE

DID YOU ORDER A PIZZA?
NO. I ORDERED A COACH WITH SIX WHITE HORSES!
DUH!
Grease Ball Pizza

ARE YOU GOING SOMEWHERE?
NO! I'M ENTERING A SUITCASE PACKING CONTEST!
TALL COOL ONE
WE'LL RETURN TO "DIVORCE COURT" AFTER THESE ANNOYING MESSAGES

WHAT'S THE PEANUT BUTTER FLAVOR LIKE?
FLAVOR OF THE MONTH
Peanut Butter
SOFT SERVE
A WILD GUESS WOULD BE A BLEND OF PEANUT BUTTER AND ICE CREAM.
SHAKE
RATTLE
ROLL
MOE'S TV'S

DR. SEUSS
~~PEDIATERICAN~~
~~PEDATRICIEN~~
BABY DOCTOR
IS THAT YOUR BABY?
NO. I RENTED HIM SO I COULD SIT HERE.
BABY WORLD
U.S. BABY & WORLD REPORT

DON'T I KNOW YOU FROM SOMEWHERE?
WINK WINK
YES. WE SHARED THE SAME NURSERY AS BABIES.
MACE

ARE YOU LOOKING FOR SOMETHING?
YES. I THOUGHT I HEARD A BURGLAR.
MOMMY
DADDY

YOU'RE NOT GOING TO HANG IT THERE, ARE YOU?
NO. I'M GOING TO HOLD IT INSTEAD.
BLESS THIS EXPENSIVE HOUSE
DISHES
LINEN
REALLY COOL

WELL, HOW ARE YOU TODAY?
JUST GREAT! IN FACT, I CAN'T WAIT TO HAVE ANOTHER ACCIDENT!
PING
PING
$50,00

WHAT'S THIS!?
IT'S A PRESENT FOR YOU TO GIVE TO ME.

DO YOU THINK THE BIRDS WILL FIND IT?
NO. I BETTER PUT AN AD IN THE PAPER.

HOW DO YOU FEEL ABOUT GOING TO JAIL?
JUST GREAT! IT'S A DREAM COME TRUE!
WNUT

CAN I GET THIS IN BLUE?
SURE. JUST TAKE IT TO OUR PAINT DEPARTMENT.
SALE!! 100% OFF
YOU WISH

BOOK
TORE
10 WEEKS ON THE
BEST SELLERS LIST
"SMART COMEBAC
FOR STUPID QUES
ARE YOU CLOSING?
HOURS
9-5
NO. THIS MEANS THE BOOKS ARE CLOSED.
CLOSED
Yes!
WE DO HAVE ESPRESSO

DID I DO SOMETHING WRONG?
NOT IF YOU MEANT TO HIT IT!
EXCELLO DRIVING ACADEMY

TITLES BY CCC PUBLICATIONS

PARTY / CARTOON BOOKS - Retail $4.99 - $6.99

101 SIGNS/SPENDING TOO MUCH TIME W/ CAT
ARE WE DYSFUNCTIONAL YET?
ARE YOU A SPORTS NUT?
BETTER HALF, The
BOOK OF WHITE TRASH, The
BUT OSSIFER, IT'S NOT MY FAULT
CAT OWNER'S SHAPE-UP MANUAL
CYBERGEEK IS CHIC
DIFFERENCE BETWEEN MEN & WOMEN, The
FITNESS FANATICS
FLYING FUNNIES
GOLFAHOLICS
GOOD FOR NOTHIN' MEN
GO TO HEALTH!
IF MEN HAD BABIES...
LOVE & MARRIAGE & DIVORCE
LOVE DAT CAT
MALE BASHING: WOMEN'S FAVORITE PASTIME
MARITAL BLISS & OTHER OXYMORONS
MORE THINGS YOU CAN DO WITH A USELESS MAN
OFFICE FROM HELL, The
OH BABY!
PMS CRAZED: TOUCH ME AND I'LL KILL YOU!
SLICK EXCUSES FOR STUPID SCREW-UPS
SMART COMEBACKS FOR STUPID QUESTIONS
SO, YOU'RE GETTING MARRIED
SO, YOU'RE HAVING A BABY
TECHNOLOGY BYTES!
THINGS/DO WITH/USELESS MAN "G-Rated"
THINGS YOU'LL NEVER HEAR THEM SAY
WHY GOD MAKES BALD GUYS
WHY MEN ARE CLUELESS
YOUR COMPUTER THINKS YOU'RE AN IDIOT

GAG / BLANK BOOKS - Retail $4.99 - $5.99

ALL/WAYS MEN/SMARTER THAN WOMEN (blank)
ALL/WAYS WOMEN/SMARTER THAN MEN (blank)
COMPLETE GUIDE/RETIREMENT'S GREAT ACTIVITIES
COMPLETE GUIDE TO SEX AFTER 30 (blank)
COMPLETE GUIDE TO SEX AFTER 40 (blank)
COMPLETE GUIDE TO SEX AFTER 50 (blank)
COMPLETE GUIDE TO SEX AFTER BABY (blank)
COMPLETE GUIDE TO SEX AFTER MARRIAGE (blank)
COMPLETE GUIDE TO OVER-THE-HILL SEX (blank)
LAST DIET BOOK, The (gag)

AGE RELATED / OVER THE HILL - Retail $4.99 - $6.99

30 - DEAL WITH IT
40 - DEAL WITH IT
50 - DEAL WITH IT
60 - DEAL WITH IT
OVER THE HILL - DEAL WITH IT!
CRINKLED & WRINKLED
RETIREMENT: THE GET EVEN YEARS
SENIOR CITIZEN'S SURVIVAL GUIDE, The
WELCOME TO YOUR MIDLIFE CRISIS
YIKES, IT'S ANOTHER BIRTHDAY
YOU KNOW YOU'RE AN OLD FART WHEN...
YOUNGER MEN ARE BETTER THAN RETIN-A

MINI BOOKS (4 x 6) Retail $4.99 - $6.99

"?" [question mark book]
IT'S A MAD MAD MAD SPORTS WORLD
LITTLE BOOK OF CORPORATE LIES, The
LITTLE BOOK OF ROMANTIC LIES, The
LITTLE INSTRUCTION BOOK OF RICH & FAMOUS
NOT TONIGHT DEAR, I HAVE A COMPUTER
OLD, FAT, WHITE GUY'S GUIDE TO EBONICS, The
SINGLE WOMEN vs. MARRIED WOMEN
TAKE A WOMAN'S WORD FOR IT

TRADE PAPERBACKS Retail $4.99 - $7.99

50 WAYS TO HUSTLE YOUR FRIENDS
1001 WAYS TO PROCRASTINATE
ABSOLUTE LAST CHANCE DIET BOOK
BOTTOM HALF, The
EVERYTHING I KNOW/LEARNED/TRASH TALK TV
GETTING OLD SUCKS!
GETTING EVEN W/ ANSWERING MACH
GREATEST ANSWERING MACHINE MESSAGES
HOW TO ENTERTAIN PEOPLE YOU HATE
HOW TO GET FREE FOOD IN COLLEGE
HOW TO REALLY PARTY!
HOW TO SURVIVE A JEWISH MOTHER
HOW TO TALK/WAY OUT OF/TRAFFIC TICKET
IT'S BETTER/OVER THE HILL THAN UNDER IT
I WISH I DIDN'T...
KILLER BRAS
LADIES, START YOUR ENGINES
LIFE'S MOST EMBARRASSING MOMENTS
HORMONES FROM HELL
HORMONES FROM HELL II
HUSBANDS FROM HELL
MEN LOVE FOOTBALL/WOMEN LOVE FOREPLAY
NEVER A DULL CARD
PEOPLE WATCHER'S FIELD GUIDE
RED HOT MONOGAMY
SHARING THE ROAD WITH IDIOTS
UGLY TRUTH ABOUT MEN
UNOFFICIAL WOMEN'S DIVORCE GUIDE
WHAT DO WE DO NOW?? (New Parents)
WHY MEN DON'T HAVE A CLUE
WORK SUCKS!

"ON THE EDGE" - Retail $4.99 - $6.99

ART OF MOONING, The
COMPLETE BOOGER BOOK, The
COMPLETE WIMP'S GUIDE TO SEX, The
FARTING
SEX AND YOUR STARS
SEX IS A GAME
SEXY CROSSWORD PUZZLES
SIGNS YOUR SEX LIFE IS DEAD
THE TOILET ZONE
THINGS/DO WITH/USELESS MAN "R-Rated"
TOTAL BASTARD'S GUIDE TO GOLF, The
YOU KNOW HE'S/WOMANIZING SLIMEBALL WHEN...